My Life As Your Sister

Jaimie Gross

PUBLISHING GROUP

First Printing, 2014
ISBN-13: 978-0990648000
ISBN-10: 0990648001
Written To Write Publishing Group, LLC
532 Metomen Street
Ripon, Wisconsin, 54971, USA
www.writtentowrite.com

Acknowledgements

I would like to thank all those involved in making this book a reality. Without these people, it would still be a document on my computer.

Eric Baierl, thank you for putting up with my crazy self for photographing the cover. Also, thank you for dealing with formatting the book. I'll try not to have another insane manuscript full of tabs and italics.
Steven Gross, thank you for writing the introduction. As always, you're a man of few words, and what you say seems to be perfect for the situation. Thank you for letting me use Teagan's photo as my cover and title page.
Teagan Gross, thank you for modeling for my cover. I will never forget the moment you realized there were bugs on the tree. Well, at least not until I am senile.
Dylan Gross, thank you for letting me use Teagan's photo as my cover and title page. I believe your husband thinks you can read minds... Maybe that is why he didn't mention the photo shoot right away.
Jeff Chen, thank you for putting together my cover. I am very grateful for your ability to interpret my awesome instructions. "Make it prettyful" is going to be my new theme.
Julie Phelps, thank you for not throwing my manuscript into the garbage. As an editor, you have a very thankless job. I'm grateful to have someone knowledgeable to shape up my manuscript.
Kim Bahr, thank you for encouraging me to look at self-publishing again. I have learned so much from this project that I would never have learned if you had not suggested having a look at it.
Debbie Gross, I wouldn't be writing if it weren't for you. There is no amount of gratitude that I can really express for you without sounding false.

My Life as Your Sister

Introduction

Dear readers,

I am the author's older brother. I have a beautiful wife and natural disaster (also known as daughter). When asked to write the introduction for this book, I didn't know what to say. Every family has difficulty with a variety of things and for kids it can be very hard to grow up separately.

By the time I read my sister's poem, I had been around the world and back a couple of times. I had gained some valuable perspective on life. This is a story of a difficult time in our family's life. It helped shape who we have become. But it hasn't defined us, and for that I am thankful because I don't know how much more time-out I can handle.

Enjoy the book,
Steven Gross

I

Welcome home Fools

We both made it home
        from school.
You're thirteen,
        I'm eleven
        and our parents are
        divorced.
While I stand high
        on a hill
        bathed in the sun's warm glow,
        you glower at
        my tiny figure.
You're encased in the dark shadow
        of a tree
        down at the bottom

of the hill.
Is it fair?
    You ask
    with anger apparent
    in your narrowed brown eyes,
That she should get the attention?
Today we step off that
    big yellow bus
    and when you try
    to help me with my homework
    I get irritated,
    I shove you away
    and I yell for Mom.
You get in trouble and
    I laugh on the inside,
    happy to see
    you in your predicament.
This is life.
Is it not?
As you get mad at me
    for being a brat
    I find ways to frame
    you more and more just to
    get you yelled at -
I want the attention.
The attention is mine.
This is what I do:
    it is my job,
    I am your sister,
    I am your sibling

I will find ways to torture
your life
and see that you
aren't as special as me
in the eyes of our family
because I am young,
I really don't understand
what loss is like.
I really don't know
        exactly how much
        you mean to me
        so I watch you frown,
        I watch you scowl
        at the wall in the corner
        of Mom's tiny kitchen
        where you stare and stare,
        try with all your might
        to burn a hole in the wall
        with your eyes...
But it isn't working
        and you are stuck
        in time-out,
        punished!
And I giggle my giggle,
        my mischievous giggle,
        the one that lets you know
        that I did this on purpose.
But what can I do?
        is what you wonder...
She always gets her way.

3

Even when we are at Dad's
        you know I can get
        you easily into trouble
        because I'm that good -
All I have to do
        is press out some tears,
        stain my cheeks
        with those salty rivers
        and fake a cry
        and then you growl
        your frustration out
        because I have won
        and you have not
        and you are still stuck
        in that corner,
        staring at the wall,
        still in trouble
        because of me -
Which is what I like.
You start to fail.
As days go by
        your grades are slipping,
        one by one,
        and now you yell
        and Mom yells back
        but you don't care...
Do you?
You're pushing the line,
        trailing the boundaries,
        trying to see

just how far you can go,
how much you can push
Mom before she snaps.
You're in seventh grade now,
you're failing really bad!
You're not even trying,
you obviously don't care
Now you've pushed Mom's
last button
and she snaps and she yells
You won't do this again!
Go live with your Dad.
I really don't care!
Perhaps he can do some good,
I hope he can help you there!
But her tears contradict
the words that she's saying.
Those hot salty tears
are flowing down
her cheeks
and they won't stop,
not for a long time.
I listen to her shout
from the closet in the hall
where I can hear everything
through the crack in the stairs.
You're downstairs
with Dad and Mom
and I'm supposed
to be asleep -

But I cannot sleep.
My childish curiosity calls
        so I must obey.
I must know
        exactly what they say
        to you downstairs
        and what I hear
        almost makes me cheer!
Pack up your things,
This will not be fun.
I'm taking you home with me.
That is the sum of
        what Dad said
        and when he said it
        I almost laughed -
You will be gone,
I'll be alone!
The attention is all mine!!
I don't have to share.
Good riddance to you anyway,
        I really don't care.
Stay with Dad,
        never come back.
I don't want to see you.
Now that I am alone,
        there's so much to do!
I'll get so much more things,
        than ever did you!
I could hear Mom crying
        the night that you left

but I didn't care.
I was happy now
 with you not there!
My eagerness peaks...
 now that I'm alone.
Mom cries each night.
 I know it,
 I hear it,
 I see the stains
 blemishing her cheeks,
But she doesn't
 tell me she's sad.
No matter how many times
 I try to cheer her up,
 it is no use...
I see the sorrow
 left in her eyes,
 stuck there since the day
 you left for your
 new home.
And I feel a bit
 guilty at first
 because I can't help but think
 that it is my fault,
 that I chased you away
 with my mischievous deeds
 to constantly get
 you into trouble
 and I think that you are
 mad at me.

But I don't let this get to me
No, I don't let it
        because I am a ruler
        of my own self!
I command my emotions
I say how I will feel
        so I pack it away -
        that dreadful guilt -
        that I felt momentarily
And I smile and say
        with my tiny hand on her cheek
        in a comforting manner.
Or, at least, so I think.
Mommy don't cry.
Give me a smile.
He went away,
He doesn't care.
But Mommy don't worry.
I love you still.
Even though he won't,
I always will.
But this only makes
        the tears fill her eyes.
She looks so sad,
        like she's going to cry.
I don't like this.
I look away.
I leave her to go
        outside to play.
I am a coward.

Yes, it is true.
I already know this,
        now so do you.
I hate to see
        when my Mom cries
        but she kept in those tears
She didn't let them go
They never passed the barriers
        of her closed lids.
She is strong you see?
Something in me says
        she is not weak,
She really is not.
If she were weak,
        then why doesn't she cry?
Why doesn't she let those tears
        just fall past her eyes?
Because she is strong,
She's stronger than you.
She's something you can never
        and never will be.
Because you're a coward,
Can't look her in the eye.
Not when she's crying.
I wonder why?
Your brother would be able
        to look her in the eye.
Even when she's crying
        and he'd apologize.
What you said was mean.

9

What you said was wrong.
But obviously you're dumb
        because you don't understand...
No, you don't even know
        how harmful those few words
were.
How stupid you are
        to think that you could
        be better than him!
All you do is harm
You never do good
Just give it up
Silence your mouth
No one wants to hear
What you have to say.
No one cares...
Not really, anyway.
That snide voice
        inside my mind
        irritated me because
        I knew it was right,
And since that day
        it has always been
        right there to laugh at me,
        to ridicule every
        mistake that I made
But what could I do
        to silence its speech?
I sat atop the jungle gym
        out in the back yard

10

and I listened to it quietly,
My mouth closed for once.
I decided that now
    would be a good time
    to silence
    the voice
    that spoke in my head.
Who it was,
    I did not know
    so I demanded of it
    to tell me who
    it was
    but it stayed silent.
It didn't seem to be there.
I wanted to cry!
I wanted to scream!
I wanted to throw something,
    And throw something I did...
    I picked up the baseball
    you always played with,
    throwing it as hard
    as I possibly could!
My aim was for the closest thing
    to me -
    about five feet away
    the propane tank stood.
I threw it hard
    and missed by a mile,
    so instead I settled for
    childishly sticking my tongue out

at the propane tank and then
I ran into the house,
grabbing a Popsicle
to cheer myself up
and I ate it happily,
glad you weren't there,
because when you weren't
I didn't have to share
since it was the last one.
I was exceptionally pleased
so I dropped the wrapper
onto the floor
not caring that Mom
was soon going to know
that it was me who did it,
that I took the Popsicle
without permission
and supper was soon
going to be made
and I would ruin my appetite
for corn dogs and French fries,
the meal that we were having
that night.
The voice came back
at supper briefly
when Mom was lecturing me
about how I should not
eat ice cream
before supper
because it ruins your meal.

The voice gave a laugh
and it told me with glee
If you had just asked me
I could have told you that!
You're so ignorant
it makes me cry.
There's so much you have
yet to learn.
My work is cut out for me.
I pity myself
for having to teach
someone such as yourself.
As I was about to yell
to tell it to quiet its mouth...
I felt its presence
disappear from my mind...
It was no longer there
so yelling would not help.
Mom's eyes were on me.
She was giving me a glare
that told me everything
and nothing at all
all at once
But I knew
exactly what she wanted
me to do.
The look in her eye
hardened to know
the fact that I had
ice cream on my mouth.

I'm a messy eater
Can you not tell?
But the sad thing is,
      well, to me anyway,
      when I didn't eat my dinner
      she sent me away...
I was then in my room
      sitting on my bed,
      already tucked in
      my teeth brushed
      my pajamas on.
There was no getting out
      of my punishment
      because
You were not there,
Brother,
You were not there
      so I could blame
      you for my actions.
Oh what a shame -
      I hated to know
      I had to take action for
      the wrapper I had thrown
      carelessly on the floor.
So now I was in
      my canopy bed
      pondering upon
      the things the voice said
Oh, yes, I was silent.
Dangerously so.

14

My mom poked her head in
     the room just to know
     to be sure I was alive still
     since I never shut up,
     my mouth is always running
     and if it is not
     I'm either dead or asleep
     because even when I eat
     while I stuff my face
     with as much food as I can
     I'm talking and gabbing,
     running my mouth
     telling everyone and anyone
     all about myself.
So it came as a surprise
     when my Mom looked inside
     my room to find
     I was still awake
     at nine o'clock at night,
     my eyes fixed on the ceiling,
     hands folded behind my head.
I'm relaxed
     just thinking
     but I don't really notice
     my mom is standing there
     in the doorway
     arms folded across her chest
     in a look of disapproval.
She quietly asks
     Why are you awake,

young lady?
I told you to sleep.
Now I expect you to be
        when I come back.
You have school tomorrow
        and you will go
        even if you're tired,
        I'll have you know!
I'm not going to let you
        stay home and sleep
        just because you wouldn't
        listen to me.
Now close those blue eyes
        and keep them that way.
I know you'll thank me
        for this one day.
I love you my child.
You and your brother are my life.
So go to sleep,
I'll wake you in the morning.
        and you better get up,
        don't you dare argue.
One word of disagreement
        and I'll time-out you.
Goodnight,
Sweetheart.
        I'm going to bed, too.
And with that
        Mom closed the door.
I closed my eyes

16

and did as she asked.
I closed my eyes
        for some much needed rest.
Though the voice wasn't there
        its words still plagued me
        and I was forced
        to wonder about it.
I didn't get far
        in my ponderings, though,
        because sleep encased me
        in its comfortable arms
        and took me away
        to dream land
        where I was content -
No voice to plague me.
But I saw my brother
        in my dreams that night.
My mom was there
        and so was my dad
Yes, I considered them mine,
        not yours as well
        because who got the attention?
Certainly not you!
I did everything I could
        to be sure you were
        kept in the shadows
        of that tall dark tree,
        jealous and wanting
        all the attention for me.
My dream was this:

I stood to the side
not really by anyone.
I felt alone
but it was just a dream.
Could I really feel?
You held Mom's hand,
a carefree young boy.
Dad came along
and held out his hand
to you, not to me!
So I was angered by this
but I saw you run
away from Mom
leaving her hand
to feel cold and empty.
Instead you took
Dad's hand and turned
your head away
not looking at Mom
as she fell to her knees
and sobbed in her hands,
But I could not run to her,
I could not comfort her,
I was rooted to the spot
and then I woke up
remembered you were gone.
You would not be coming home.
I felt jealous!
I felt angry!
I knew I had to get you back

18

so I could torture
every moment of your life!
But that wouldn't happen,
this much I knew,
so I needed another plan
and hoped one would grow
and blossom into an infallible plot
to get you back
into my life.
But nothing came.
Nothing at all.
I am stuck here now,
lost and alone.
So now I must suffer
until I find
a way to get to you -
Perhaps it will work
and I will smile again
Get you in trouble.
because that is my job.
It is what I do.
Don't you know that yet?
I was so sure you did.
Well, maybe someday I'll tell you
but just not right now...
I'll keep you in the dark,
without a clue
and you'll take my blame
Yes, soon things will be the same
as they always were.

II

Goodbye Irritant!!
You're leaving me
Yay!
You won't be here,
      the attention is mine!
A day goes by
      but you are at Dad's.
You'll like it there,
      to live without me,
But another day goes by
      and a week and a month
      and I get bored
      without you here.
Who to annoy?
      I think to myself

Mom? Step Dad?
No, that won't do,
There is no one as fun
    to annoy as there is you.
What I must admit
    is that you are my brother
    and my sole purpose in life
    is to annoy you.
Only you.
You don't feel privileged?
Well why not?
The voice came back to me
    snide as it ever was
    and pointed something out to me
    I hadn't thought before
Why would he feel privileged?
You're just a brat
    as bad as a gnat.
And don't you know?
No one likes a gnat.
So that's why he doesn't feel
    'privileged' as you say
    because you're a pest.
Someone should have called
    the exterminators a long time ago
    and put you to sleep,
Buried you six feet under
    rather than fix
    that hole in your heart
    because all it was

was a waste of money.
You are worth even less than a penny!
So you see,
> *when you ask*
> *if he feels privileged*
> *you should ask yourself*
> *how you would feel*
> *if you were in the same*
> *situation as he*
> *because now he's alone.*
Not that he'd mind
> *because anything is better*
> *than spending a day with you.*
You realize that right?
I sure hope you do.
If you can't understand this
> *I'll admit defeat.*
You're a hopeless case,
> *which I gladly drop at my feet.*
And then the voice left
> as quick as it came,
> leaving me much to think about
> pressing you further into my
thoughts.
It bothered me
> to think so much
> about you because
> I was rid of you
> and I wanted it to stay
> that way because I was sure

that I was happy.
I am right?
To have nothing to do
day or night?
My grades had been slipping
since you had left
because now you were not there
to help me out,
to teach me to understand
what I couldn't comprehend,
since you'd learned this stuff already...
it came easy to you...
When you'd help me out
even though I seemed to resent you,
getting you into trouble
so often each day.
But now you weren't there
I couldn't say
Hey!
Big brother will you
come help me with this?
I don't understand -
I've made a mistake -
I'm sure I have -
This work is so hard.
It wouldn't be hard
to convince you to help
but without you there
and since Mom didn't know
at all how to help

and I couldn't ask Step Dad
because he was at work
doing whatever
it was that he did.
So I just sat back
and watched the failing grades
get worse and worse
and then realized
the tiniest thing.
It brought a smile to my face.
I knew what to do -
no, not with my homework
But it was about you.
I knew how to get
myself by you
to go to live
with Dad
So I can smile and laugh
as I get you into trouble
once more.
Because I had realized
just what you did,
or more accurately,
Didn't.
You didn't do your homework.
You failed in your schoolwork.
So I started that too
I started to form
my plan
that was so eager to grow.

I sat in my classroom,
        my fifth grade math class.
At first I had been excelling
I was in the advanced fifth grade math
        so I slowly let a grin
        spread across my face
        and started to turn in
        work that was wrong,
Work not completely done,
        and I watched the teacher's smile
        turn fast into a frown.
Oh well.
I thought
My plan will work.
I will be over there
        annoying you soon
        so just wait for me, brother
I'm coming for you.
Soon I was switched
        to the lower math class,
Because I couldn't understand
        was their excuse,
Psh, yeah, right!
If you tried you would...
But I ignored that small fact
The voice had just said
I wouldn't agree;
I wouldn't dare;
At least not out loud
        and soon I found myself
26

out in the hallway
My teacher standing
        in front of me
        with a scowl on her face
You're just like him!
        she said with a frown,
You really don't care!
If you don't get a better attitude
        I'll call your mother
        I'm sure you don't want that!
I just sat through the lecture
        my face void of emotions.
I wouldn't admit
        the fact that I didn't like
        being compared to you,
Just like that.
It raked my nerves
Just those few words
        and I found myself
        increasingly angry
        as she continued her speech
        about how you were the same,
        and what I was doing
        to be like you...
So this was how
        I began to grow up.
When I was talked to
        by someone I didn't want
        to listen to
        I just sat there

pretending I didn't have ears.
I didn't want to know
       what I had already heard.
I would smile
       but that wasn't how I truly felt.
Not at the time.
Most of the time.
I felt angry.
Upset.
Hurt.
To be compared to you,
       my greatest ally
       but also my greatest foe.
I found myself with less
       friends than before
       which is hard to do
       when you started with none.
In ninth grade I found
       myself with no friends,
       and the friends I did have
       were backstabbing jerks
Using me for things
       like gel pens and money
       which hurt a lot
       though I knew it would happen.
The voice had told me
       that it would.
Because of my actions
       and the way I held myself,
It told me that I

would have to change
But I refused to do so,
    not wanting to give up
    the plan that had
    yet to work.
I frowned and
    silenced my words,
    speaking to no one
    who I thought undeserving
    because I was angry
    with myself and with others.
Mainly myself.
Because I was naïve
    and I seemed to think
    the world would be perfect
To me -
A brat -
A spoiled brat.
I had to have my way though,
    so I silenced my voice...
I said no more,
    not for four weeks.
The only ones I talked to
    were my family
    because I couldn't escape
    my mother who'd yell
    at me for ignoring her
    and not answering her questions.
This is stupid.
The voice said:

you are stupid.
He wouldn't do this,
       so why do you?
Are you trying to prove something?
If you are
       you are doing a very bad job
Just like you do
       a bad job at everything else.
So give it up,
       give it a rest,
Have a good cry,
Get it off your chest.
You know you want to
       with the way these people treat
you
So why don't you do it?
The voice disappeared...
I knew it did
But I answered it anyway
       not speaking aloud.
It was bad enough
       to be treated how I was.
I didn't want people calling me
       'Schizophrenic' too
To add to all the names
       I was already called.
Because I am not weak,
I do not cry,
I'm not the little girl
I used to be.
30

I can hold back my tears
        just like my Mom,
So leave me alone
        you stupid, dumb voice!
You don't understand me!
You never will!
I'm always misunderstood
        especially by you!
In those four weeks,
Though you'll never guess
        a glare crept into my face
        and it scared some people
        to add to the names
I was already called -
Was 'evil eyes' and 'schizophrenic'
Because I would glare at
        anyone who offended me.
I would sit there and stare,
        burn a hole in their head
        with my eyes
        and they would shift in their seat
        and they would still have
        the audacity to laugh
One day I was furious
        at a boy who had laughed
        called me a few names
        and I stood up quickly,
        somehow knocking over
        my desk
And I glared at the boy

31

for a moment or two
while he laughed with his friends
and said jeering words
And that was the moment
that I went ballistic
screaming at him
yelling at him
not noticing the tears streaming
down my face
saying whatever came to mind...
The teacher came back from
the errand he'd run
and saw the fight,
deciding to join in on the fun...
What's going on here?
he asked with a sigh.
A few stragglers pointed
to my lithe figure
and I scowled at the one
who decided to speak:
She started it all.
the helpful girl said
and I promised to get my
revenge on this girl,
Briefly wondering just
what you were doing
before the teacher took my arm,
dragging me into the hall.
So there I was
in the hall with the teacher

He was obviously not happy.
So what?
Neither was I!
Here I was
        getting in trouble
For the nasty things said
        to me
        and I had to deal with
        most likely a detention -
Or two -
Or three -
Four, if I was lucky.
Oh joy.
I thought
I swear if I get
        reamed for this
        I will slug him in the face
        And then skip the day away.
But he didn't yell at me
        except to say
I know you're having trouble
        with the other students.
I don't know what was going on
        but I want you to know
        I'm on your side.
Truth to tell,
His words didn't comfort me.
My initial thought was
        Gee thanks.
If you were on my side

why the heck am I
the one in the hall
when he was the one
who started it all?
But the teacher continued,
        the frown still in place:
Why don't you go
        to the library and wait?
I'll call the librarian
        and tell them you're to be there
        and you can wait
        to calm yourself down.
Whenever you're ready
        you can just come back.
The only emotion
        I showed him that day,
        other than the tear streaks
        swelling my cheeks,
        was a frown and a nod
        since I wouldn't admit
        my respect towards him
        had gone up a bit.
I left to the library.
My stuff in his room -
I would pick it up later
        after his class
        after the people have
        all gone away.
I stayed through that class
        and also the next

in a side room of the
library.
No one noticed me.
No one seemed to care.
I just sat and sat
having a conversation in my
mind
with the voice who had returned
to bother me again:
Well that was something!
the voice said with glee.
*I never thought that
someone like you
would have the guts to
stick up for yourself.
You proved me wrong!
Perhaps you're not hopeless…
I suppose we'll see soon.*
I frowned and I glared at the voice
which is impossible to do
since the voice was in my head
but I managed it anyway,
Or at least I'm sure I did
since it backed off when I said
*Why are you always here?
Why do you care?
You're less wanted in my mind
than I am at this school.
Everyone hates me,
that's obvious to me now.*

For once the voice's presence
     did not disappear
The moment I started to speak
     to vanish into thin air.
So it seemed to stay
As it said
I'm only here
     because you're here
I'm a part of you.
There is no escape.
Wherever you go,
     I will be there.
I'm the one person
     who you can count on
     other than yourself
     to help you get through.
So I come when I'm needed
     or else when I choose.
You made me the day
     your brother left to go
     so now you must realize
     that I'm here to stay
My frown deepened
     when I thought of those words.
I wondered if they
     could possibly be true...
If the voice was a part of me
     then why did I want it to go
away?
I wiped the tears away

not wanting to cry anymore.
I looked at my hands
　　　　and then looked to the floor.
I smiled then
　　　　as I spoke to the voice
　　　　keeping my words in my head
I'm proud of myself...
It could have been worse...
My first time to talk to them
　　　　in four whole weeks...
And I actually blew up...
Screamed all my feelings -
The voice laughed
　　　　and I snickered.
I was happier than I had been.
You did well,
The voice told me
　　　　and I heard pride in the voice.
I didn't really care
　　　　that I was holding a conversation
　　　　with a voice in my head
Which was just really odd
　　　　but I kept up the conversation
　　　　which I held in my head
　　　　and the voice didn't leave me
　　　　like it always did before.
It stayed there with me
　　　　until I fell asleep on the floor
　　　　curled up in the corner
　　　　to sleep away the lunch hour

only to wake again
when the librarian woke me
telling me that I had missed
two extra classes.
I shrugged that off
feeling really good,
Went and picked up my books
and went to my next class,
Not bothering to notice
that same boy was in my class,
Not bothering to notice that boy
was still there,
jeering and sneering
having a good laugh
being an idiot
with his friends.
I didn't really care,
not with the voice there
and I was pleased to find
that it had not left
It stuck with me
like a true friend would have
if I had friends.

III

See you later, Fool
You're off to boot camp!
You've graduated,
      you're done,
      you could start a new life,
      but surprisingly enough
      we've grown closer this last year...
You talk to me,
      you listen to me
      like no one else would.
I can't consider
      you to be my friend
      because you're my brother.
There can't be more.
There can't be less.

We're enemies,
  we're allies,
  all at the same time
  but no one else realizes this.
No one but me
  and the voice who resides
  inside my head.
You want to know something?
The voice said to me,
  I think you have grown up
  at least a little bit
I'm proud of you for that.
I smiled to myself.
When I watched you graduate
  you got your diploma
  all dressed up in red
  and the voice said to me
Well, now what to do?
He's gone and graduated
  and will soon leave your Dad's home.
So how will you react?
Your plan failed
  I hope you'll admit.
I think you should give up on it.
I nodded my head.
I looked at your face
  and I watched you grin.
I don't think I will
  give up on my plan.
I don't like my school.
40

I need a change,
> *I want to wear red,*
> *I want to start over*
Where rumors are no longer
> *able to hurt me*
> *and no one calls me*
> *those despicable names.*
So I think I will continue -
No reason to stop
> *just because he's graduated*
> *and I am not.*
I let my life fail
> without you there
> to poke and prod
> and thoroughly upset me,
> keep me on track...
So I gave up long ago
> when you left me to go
> to live with our Dad
> and leave me feeling sad
> when I realized what I
> had lost:
> a brother to bother
But I don't let it show
> because now you are gone
> and though I still fail
> you're in boot camp
> right now.
So what do I do?
Soon you'll come home

and I'll spend
time with you
but before you come back
Grandpa will die
and I will be left
all alone as I cry,
hating my weakness,
hating the tears
that spring to my eyes
And I wish I were strong again
just like Mom,
able to keep them back
But it is just too much for me.
The voice comforts me
soothes me
tells me everything will be okay
But I feel something in me break
because my grandpa has died
And a special trip to my dad's house -
An emergency trip -
was taken
just so that Dad could tell me
the bad news.
I had asked Mom
on the way to Dad's
What, did Grandpa die?
in a sarcastic tone.
It might have been easier to handle
had it not been Dad who told me
but his eyes were filled with grief

and I could see clearly he was pained
by the loss of his father
and I hated it.
I didn't want to see it.
Didn't want to know it.
And you were not here to tell me
that everything would be okay,
the God that Grandpa had
believed in so much
had let him die.
I had prayed
when I found out
Grandpa's health was failing,
I had prayed so hard!
Every day!
But it is obvious now
that my prayers went on deaf ears
so I cried myself into oblivion
for the next few weeks
seeing Grandpa
And only him
in my dreams.
No one noticed...
Not at all...
that I was tortured
by the loss.
I was more 'Grandpa's girl' than
I was 'Daddy's girl' or
'Momma's girl'
I loved my grandpa!

I loved him so much!
      but the person I loved most
      died
      so I don't believe in God!
Not anymore!
And did anyone think
That I might want to talk to him
      before he died??
Obviously not!
And that hurt a lot -
      so I cried
      and cried
      and felt extremely weak
      and I hated that you
      could not be there
      to have closure at the funeral
So I didn't go get my own closure.
I didn't approach the casket
      and at times I am thankful
      that I did not
      because from what slight
      glimpses I caught
      I knew
      Grandpa would not have wanted
      us to see him
      looking as frail as he did
      just then.
But then I will see
      you go away again.
I'm left to hang

on an invisible thread
All alone again
except for the voice
that resides in my head.
Iraq, here you come
You're over there now...
Doing what?
I wonder.
Losing the boy
that you grew up with
until you were eleven
and he left you alone
to struggle, to strive
to live, to survive.
The voice told me one day
I smiled and shook my head.
He did me a favor,
he just doesn't know it.
Someday I'll tell him
but just not right now.
Right now, I will sit here
all pretty in my chair
and pretend he's sitting there
right across from my chair.
I told the voice happily
now you shoot, blast, and blow
those Iraqi people
to Hell and more!
I can hardly hide
the horror I feel

so I hide behind myself...
withdraw myself...
Slowly burn in a dying fire
inside me.
As I hear news of you
it sickens me, pains me
angers me
to watch you come home
and see your eyes are -
Believe it or not -
a shade darker than before,
filled with secrets
you wish to hide
probably not just from me.
These secrets you may want
just to forget
or memories you want to
hold onto forever,
Cherish or loathe.
These things that you know.
You know more than we do.
You might not want to talk
about it ever again.
Or you might want to.
but you don't know what to say.
But each glance you give me
each time you look at me
I find less heart to look into
Your eyes,
not wanting to see

what I realize isn't there.
And then you go away again
        bound for Japan.
I'm shamed to be thankful
        to know you will go.
        another day of your eyes -
        I know I would scream!
But does anyone understand?
No.
I'm always misunderstood.
So I keep silent
Don't tell my own secret:
I want you gone.
I feel ashamed
        but I have to admit
This is horribly true
        so while you are in Japan
        I beat myself up
        hating that I felt glad
        about you being gone -
But your eyes,
        they still haunt me!
I tell myself:
        I'm evil
But the voice denies it:
        No you aren't,
        you're misunderstood.
I began to curse at you secretly
        because I could see your eyes
        each time I blinked.

You're there,
I can't be rid of you
        even though you're in Japan
On the other side of the world.
I write more and more,
        not that I didn't write before
        because when Grandpa died
        I finished one book.
I'm just trying to write away
        your pestering eyes...
I can't...
        they're there still...
Word arrives:
        you're back in Iraq.
Angry, I absorb myself
        in my writing.
I am content,
        able to do whatever I want:
Create worlds
        alternate universes
        places no one expects to find.
I expand myself further
        writing scenarios I can only hope
        are as real lives as possible
I give my characters
        horrible lives,
        working hard at properly
        toning their emotions.
My school grades slip -
        Again.

48

Big surprise?
But grandpa is dead
        and you arc in Iraq
        so I don't care
One moment I'm at Mom's
        the next I'm at Dad's
Mom pours out tears
        but I look away again.
I don't want to see,
        I am afraid!
Who knows how you feel?
Right now you're in Iraq
        getting shot at.
I would freak out
        if I were in your shoes.
The voice doesn't disagree.
It stays silent.
Dad barely spares me
        a single brief glance
        for an entire month
        after I move
        except to lecture me about
        my grades.
Well, that's no surprise
I expected no less
        but who would have thought
        as she headed for bed
        that very first night...
Guess what Step Mom said...
        I'm glad you're here.

Just those few words made
        all the difference to me
        though I still felt alone
        as I had for years.
That very first night
        many thoughts ran through my
head
        but surprisingly enough
        none were of you.
It took a while
        to fall asleep
        as I looked over my life,
        pathetic and pointless as it
        was so far.
And I knew how different
        things could be:
No more 'friends' to use me
No more 'family' to betray me
No more false praise from idiots
        who couldn't tell the difference
        between a novel and a
        frying pan if their life depended
        on it.
No more pretending I am not hurt
        by the scorn in the words said to
me
        every day
No more trying to be friends.
Now I would distance
        myself from the crowd

At first I put away my writing,
      instead favoring
      schoolwork,
      keeping ahead.
Many times I got called
      names like manipulative
      useless and fraud.
It seems I twist things
      until they're my way
      and according to Dad
      I don't even care
      so why should he bother?
Why should he try?
      I thought to myself
But if I say a word
      I know I'll get reamed
      for arguing with him.
So I put on my face -
      my 'uncaring' face -
      and pretend that I
      am anywhere but here.
Eventually I graduated
      to everyone's surprise
      except my own and the voice.
I made you proud
      and that was all that mattered -
      not Dad or Mom
      or anyone else's praise
Mattered as much as yours
      with Grandpa gone.

So I jumped for joy
        gave a loud WHOOP!
        congratulating myself
        with a pat on the back.
But shortly after
        I was pushed in the shade
        under the tree
        at the bottom of the hill
        where you used to stand.
Now I always will
        but I like it here.
        and the voice is content
        I've found my place.
I now know where I belong
        and I'll watch from afar
        as you soak up the sun
        at the top of the hill
        in your much earned attention.
My smile might fade
        into a scowl
        as you give me a cocky grin
        peering at me through your
        even darker eyes
And I will look away,
        not wanting to see
        what I know isn't there.
The boy you once were
        has grown up
And fast,
        though you might try to hide it

I know your smile won't last
and when it fades
you'll make sure you're alone.
You'll look at your hands
You'll look at the wall
You'll look at your feet
        but you won't stop them all,
Those tears that will come
        in a day or in years.
You have been affected.
Don't think I don't know -
        I'm your baby sister.
It's my job to know.
I realize these things
When Dad tells me all
        I ever will do
        is destroy lives
        just like Mom
Well, then, he doesn't know
        the first thing of me
        because, just like you,
        I'll smile when I'm sad,
        unable to correct him
        and make him see right
        for fear he'll get mad
And I'll look away
        and pretend I can't hear
        though every word
        is like a slap in the face.
And I'll see your eyes again

53

        as I head off to bed
        to write.
My escape.
It's all that I have.
So the scorn cannot reach me
        and make me go mad
So, here you go brother!
        a welcome home gift
        from a fool to Dad's hero.
You do know you are!
In less than eight years
        you've accomplished that
From the shade to the sun
        because you deserve it.
I anticipate those eyes of yours
have gotten darker.
Oh well, who cares?
I'm the only one
        who notices anyway.
You're now a hero!
Dad's hero!
Praise yourself! You deserve it!
And I'm still a fool
        but now I'm happy alone
I can stand here and watch you
        soak up the sun
But I won't interfere
        though I'll be somewhat jealous.
Well, what can I say?
Old habits die hard

and all you will know
is that I can only continue
to try to make you proud,
to do my very best,
because without you
there would have been no me.
You are my brother,
one of the few beings I respect
Unconditionally.
Even when you dump cold water on
me.
Even when you laugh at me.
Even when you joke about me.
I will always say:
I hate you!
Which means
'I love you.'
Crawl into a gutter and die!
which translates as
'You're so frustrating I could
pull my hair out.'
Don't talk to me ever again!
which is code for
'Talk to me later
when I'm in a better mood.'
Get out of my face you jerk!
which means
'I really had a bad day
and I don't want to talk about it
but if you keep bugging me

I'll probably tell you my problem.'
Go away!
    which is actually
    'Please stay...'
So, brother, I would just like to say
    I hate you a lot
    and go away.

Love,
Your Baby Sister

About the author

Jaimie Gross enjoys delicious cups of tea and warm afternoon naps with her two cats, Mitsuki and Neira. Currently she lives in Ripon, Wisconsin. She works full-time at a factory and part-time everywhere else. Jaimie strongly believes that one day all her hard work will pay off... somehow.